# JONESING:

# LOVE

# AND

# ITS' AFTER

# EFFECTS

*TIMELESS*

# Jonesing: Love & Its After Effects

Printed in the United States of America

**ISBN-13: 978-0692215562**
**ISBN-10: 0692215565**

Printed by Createspace in 2014
Published by BlaqRayn Publishing Plus in 2014

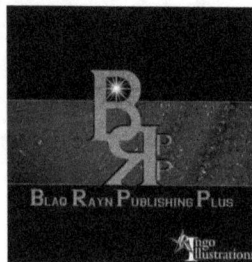

BLAQ RAYN PUBLISHING PLUS
Jngo Illustrations

# DEDICATION

Dedicated to everyone who has ever loved, lost and was bold enough to love again.

I give thanks to the Creator for endowing me with the gift to write the truths that inspire and ignite fires.  Many thanks to my mother, Nancy, for believing in me and supporting me. I thank everyone who has ever given me an encouraging word and supported my endeavor to share **ALL** of my poetry to the masses.  My hope is that this book, dedicated to the beauty of love and the pain of love, will make you reminiscence, smile and know that love, no

matter what, is the greatest gift.

*Let him kiss me with the kisses of his mouth – for your love is more delightful than wine.  Song of Solomon 1:2*

# JONESING

Jonesing

I am caught up in feeling you.

This is as lethal as heroin.

As crippling as cocaine.

In the words of Amy, "I don't want no rehab!"

I would rather chase this high no matter

where it leads me.

I am feening, scheming to get my next high.

Got to be near you.

**Jonesing**

I can't deny you've got my mind.

Preoccupied.

Tied up in thoughts of you.

Where you are.

When will I see you?

It's true; I am a fool for you.

But I have no shame.

**Jonesing**

Forced to come down off this high.

You are nowhere to be found.

Cold turkey detox.

Breaking me down.

Pitiful wails fall on deaf ears.

You're not **jonesing**.

At least not for me.

**Jonesing**

I am an addict.

Any place, anytime, anywhere you want me

to be.

I will forget everything for a chance to

experience the sweet high you give.

With each connection

The craving is greater than the cure.

I will endure

The pain of withdrawal just to keep **Jonesing**.

# TIME

Time is not on our side.

Are we blinded by the past?

Unable to get to the task of being whom we

can be to each other?

Afraid the love will not be as strong, long,

involved?

Why waste time trying to recapture what was

meant for that time?

Let's move into the now.

Savor what we have been given.

Tasting the sweet, the bitter.

Allowing it to saturate the senses.

Releasing the tension that builds because of the

words we won't say.

Sparing feelings while losing the best moments.

Spaces in time that will not return.

We won't learn that we are cosmically

intertwined.

Inexplicably in love

In spite of the separation.

Not the storybook, fairytale kind

But the familiar, passionate, perfect fit, under

my skin love.

Time is not on our side.

We know we'll decide to say good-bye if only

to stay in love.

# MEMORY

The years seem like mere moments since we

last shared an embrace and kiss.

My heart still races when we share a glance.

Memories of passionate love making that

melded fantasy and reality.

The rest of the world was irrelevant,

unimportant.

Your kiss is as familiar as the sweet scent of

fresh bread.

I will never forget how wonderful it feels to be

kissed with such tenderness and passion.

The years seem like mere moments but I am

reminded that time has passed and we have

changed.

My heart still skips a beat when I see you

stride towards me.

I anticipate the kiss we normally share.

But, your smile is not for me.

Your arms do not reach out to hold me close.

You do not whisper" I love you" close to my

ear.

I see a beautiful face lovingly look at you.

Hold your face.

Kiss you.

The years now become a bridge we no longer

cross.

Our love is a beautiful memory.

# DÉJÀ VU

It seems reasonable to believe that our spirits

have met before.

That we shared an unmatched love,

A fiery passion that consumed us.

And reached into the depths of our souls.

Somewhere in a forgotten past we lived as one.

Now when I look into your eyes I get a glimpse

of who you may have been when I was the one

your lips loved to kiss completely.

The one you held in your arms to comfort and

protect.

Do you see the woman I was to you?

The one who desired to be your one and only?

The only beautiful woman you could see.

Who used her heart, mind, body and soul to

love you.

Our smiles tell of a familiarity that is distant

but tangible.

We connect profoundly.

It is unbearable to realize that is all a fantasy.

In this earthly realm there is no place for us.

Only in the creative depths of our

imaginations can we express our connection.

Sweet déjà vu works its magic on our minds.

Giving a fleeting glimpse of a world that only

our subconscious remembers.

Reality melded into fantasy.

It is reasonable to believe that our spirits have

met before.

## TANGIBLE

Your voice caresses my spirit.

It is as tangible as the feel of your hands

touching my body.

Your smile warms my heart as deeply as any

kiss we've shared.

My thoughts of you are metaphoric.

There's beauty in all the moments we've

shared—

Joy, sadness, anger, pleasure.

Keep my hope in love alive.

It's not merely euphoria that draws me to you.

It's the familiarity; the comfort I feel in your

presence.

I can feel you in each heartbeat.

Taste you in the tears I shed.

Knowing that when you're with another our

souls still mate.

My essence of love

The most precious, sacred part belongs to you.

I freely give it to you.

I trust you to nurture and protect the

priceless gift of my love.

# IN YOUR EYES

In your eyes I see a beauty in myself I've never

nurtured.

Not a mere outer beauty.

But a feminine treasure that's been waiting for

the right moment to be found.

The right hands to handle carefully this

priceless find.

From your lips are kisses that provide a balm

to fears present and past.

Not merely kisses that arouse my flesh, but

reach deeply into my heart.

Through them words of comfort and sincerity

flow.

In your arms I am completely enveloped, held

tightly, supported.

I close my eyes and believe what I feel while

I'm there.

I hold on to the strength I know is there.

I listen to the beat of your heart and put

myself in there for the moment.

Through you I've found new hope in love.

A new zeal for life.

The certainty that you've changed my life for

the better.

# EVERY DAY

Every day is an opportunity to love you more.

Love you better than I did yesterday.

Every moment is a chance to give the best I

have.

Unselfishly putting you first.

You are unconditional love in action.

Each caress we share fills me with joy and

hope.

I know when the physical body fails.

I can lean on your love.

Pure, simple, exclamatory love to envelope me

in a loving cocoon of protection.

I never want to take for granted the love we

share so easily.

Wherever you are is where my home is.

I am most comfortable in your presence.

No one doubts the passion that lingers

between us.

We don't hide the attraction that is like fire

between us.

We want others to catch hold of just a spark

of what we share.

Love is universal.

Joy is a gift.

We welcome all who respect our love.

Who are inspired by our desire to stay true to

our bond.

Every day is an opportunity to love you more.

Love you better than I did yesterday.

Every moment is a chance to give the best I

have.

With you is where I always want to be.

Building a life together.

Taking the world by storm.

No fear of what tomorrow will bring.

Just living life to the fullest.

Enjoying this perfect gift of true love.

That brought two imperfect hearts together.

# Completely

You are the beat of my heart.

The essence of every inhale, every exhale.

I would have never dared to imagine, believe

that I would love any man the way that I love

you.

Being in love in not just a warm feeling that

makes me smile when I think of you.

It is the promise that I am loved.

I am adored.

I am cherished.

The love I give you is beyond what my body,

heart and soul can offer.

We have always shared a connection that is

intangible yet tangible.

Separated by many years yet it only seems

like moments.

An enduring love that I was unaware lay

waiting to be awakened by your voice, your

touch, your smile.

This love is a gift that I hold close.

Selfishly close.

It is obvious from the smile I wear.

The glow that I cannot subdue that something

magical is happening in my life.

Though I know that what we have is so very

special.

It is indescribable.

I want to rewind time and tell you what I

should have said so long ago.

No one has ever loved me like you.

No one has ever connected to my heart and

soul like you.

No one has ever been so incredibly kind.

Shown such unconditional love.

You are the beat of my heart.

The essence of every inhale, every exhale.

I am completely in love with you.

## SUMMER BREEZE

A summer breeze lightly blowing across my

skin reminds me of your caress.

Soothing, gentle just barely there

But filling me with sensations that bring a

smile of joy to my face to feel such comfort.

I try to hold on to the feeling as it softly drifts

away.

My skin still tingles where the breeze lightly

kissed.

My mind is consumed with the memories of

your smile, your look of passion and love.

The summer breeze that cools the day fills me

with warmth and longing to see you and

touch you.

# CAUTION TO THE WIND

Who throws caution to the wind?

A free spirit who lives only for the moment?

Or

A true spirit who lives in the moment reveling,

cherishing the intangible texture that cannot

be understood by the ordinary.

One who can find beauty in a rainy day.

One who does not need sunshine to see the

lush green of trees or the vibrant colors of

flowers.

A spirit that connects with another with a

glance and feels the tenderness of fingertips

and lips in that moment.

One who accepts the fallacies and

inconsistencies of others and believes in their

unseen potential.

Caution is of no consequence to either spirit.

The free spirit misses the message in the wind.

The true spirit leans into the wind enjoying

the wonder of its message.

## RETRACE

Retrace my steps,

Begin in your bedroom.

Put your ear close to the pillow.

You will hear my laughter.

My joy that I was there with you.

Lie in the warmth of the place you held me.

Feel the love I enveloped you.

Retrace my steps,

Remember the moments we made love.

I gave you my heart and a view of my soul.

I called your name,

Listen to the urgency.

The pleasure I received.

Each time we connected.

Retrace my steps,

Inhale the air around you.

I left my essence in that space.

I gave you a little of me each time we touched.

I wanted to pour this passion into your being.

So that you would never thirst for love again.

I wanted to be the one.


Retrace my steps,

To the door.

Down the steps.

To the street.

I am waiting for the moment.

When you embrace me and know that I am

real.

Instead you continue to search.

I slip away with the tear on your face.

## COCOA SUN

Languishing in his cocoa sun warms my heart.

It overflows with love that flows like sweet

liquid through my veins.

I will it to transfer to his soul.

I want him covered in the warm stickiness

that my love provides.

The cocoa sun never loses it rays.

They penetrate my being keeping me

enthralled and entranced by its power to

touch me lightly but stir my passion deeply.

I languish in his cocoa sun.

Basking in the healing power it brings.

Growing in the illuminating glow.

Flourishing like a beautiful flower.

Blossoming, springing forth life and vitality.

My desires are sated.

I am at ease and pleased with the results the

cocoa sun provides.

His cocoa sun rises and I bask in the ultimate

burst of pleasure it provides.

His cocoa sun sets and I relax in the slumber of

burning embers that only needs a slight breeze

to revive the full effect of his heat.

Languishing in his cocoa sun is all I need.

I exhale.

He wraps his arms around me.

I inhale.

He pulls me close.

I absorb the cocoa.

The sun.

We are one.

# KISS

I want to walk through the door and give you

a... I missed you kiss.

A long, slow kiss that pours out all the

emotions that course through my veins for you.

Not a let's make love kiss.

Just a my heart beats for the next moment I

kiss you kiss.

Look deeply into your eyes so you can see the

reflection of my joy that I love you.

I want to sit close to you and talk about

whatever comes to mind.

Uncomplicated exchanges that evoke laughter,

hugs... kisses.

I want to hold you.

Put my face against your neck and inhale your

scent.

All the while smiling because I love the smell of

your skin, the taste.

Memories are embedded in my mind of times

shared lying still.

Passion in the air but no connection of bodies.

Just me and you really connecting

metaphysically, intimately.

I want to abandon my doubts, trepidations,

insecurities and just love you.

Feel free to tell you everything that matters to

me.

Joyful, sorrowful.

I want to be completely feminine, soft.

Let you cherish me.

Not be able to live without me.


I want the forever love.

The fearless love.

The soul mate love.

I want the feel of your lips on my skin seared

into my spirit.

I want your kiss on my lips to never end.

To be awakened from the deep sleep of

resistance.

That prevents me from giving you a "I missed

you kiss".

## Time Does Not Matter

My thoughts of you are not memories of

moments we shared.

But the hope of what is to come.

The time we spend in each other's thoughts

transcends the tangible.

We have not touched or behave as lover's do.

But the time spent writing words of comfort

and encouragement equals a moment in each

other's arms.

In time we will become what our hearts

already know.

The time we've been apart will be but a

minute when we are blessed to be in each

other's presence.

Time will not dim the promise I feel when we

speak and when I think of you.

But time allows me to prepare for what my

mind says is impossible but my heart says is

real.

Time is our ally.

It has allowed us to know each other beyond

the physical.

We are metaphysical.

Soon my thoughts will be of moments we have

shared.

Time will not matter.

# DIGGING

Dark and smooth

Solid brother

Matches my passion stroke for stroke

Embraces my strength

Encourages my sensuality

Nurtures it.

Mocha on Espresso

Creating a rhythm unmatched and uncensored.

Breathless

Stretched wide unable to stifle the cries.

Ahh!

Damn!

Don't stop!

The clock seems to stop when this dark,

smooth, solid brother

brings me to the brink.

Taking me to ecstasy.

Making me dizzy and drunk on his groove.

I'm hooked.

Don't want no rehab!

I just want mocha on espresso.

Digging each other.

**YOU DIG ME**

In your eyes I see what you do not want to

reveal.

You dig me.

You want to capture the groove of my stride

You're trying to feel the glide in my hips

The mystery of my lips.

You dig me.

In my eyes you'll see the passion that burns

A heat that yearns to be unleashed.

I dig you.

You bring my body alive with your touch

Sometimes its too much

To hold the desire inside

I dig you.

The wildness of your hair.

The intent focus of your stare.

The sweet, complete satisfaction that

overcomes, subsides

Quietly contemplating the unusualness of it all

Completely carefree not held down by the

usual

Willing to taste the sweetness I provide

Proving what I already know

You dig me.

## Off Guard

It's not my habit to allow anyone into my love

space

Yet you found the tiniest opening in my tough

exterior.

Showing me that you are not deterred by my

declaration that no one is allowed in my world

without my permission.

You gently persuade me.

You see a beauty that is hidden from me

A soft, vulnerable woman who wants to be

adored but does not dare let her guard down.

A woman who is comforted by your

masculinity and virility.

The pureness of your sensuality and the

boldness of your sexuality.

I am liberated by your passion yet I hold back

because that's what I do best.

I am tied up in lost loves, heartache and

distrust.

When I am on the brink of letting go I reach

back for a taste of the bitterness that

hardened my heart.

The steady, stable beat of your heart beckons

me to trust you and that you are who God

called a man to be.

A protector, a lover and a friend.

My mind believes what my heart cannot trust

But it is not my habit to allow anyone into my

space.

# THE SCENT OF LOVE

A light breeze blew through my window

bringing with it the familiar scent of you.

I inhaled deeply and was transported back to

a time when all I wanted to do was soak you

in.

Your smile gave me joy.

Your kisses inspired passion unbridled.

The strength of your embrace gave me the

confidence to push forward.

As the breeze continues to gently caress my

skin I recall the tenderness we shared when

our love was new.

Making love, love making, quaking, Richter

scale breaking moments that made us stop in

amazement that two people could connect and

make the very core of the earth shift and line

up with the power of their love.

The light breeze reminds me that love is

strong yet fragile.

Every gesture must be treasured.

My heart is like a flower opening up to you

again.

It longs to pace itself with the strong beat that

comes from you and connects with me.

The breeze still lightly blows and the sun

warms my flesh.

Your presence is stronger.

I anticipate the breeze guiding you back to me.

Love is never far away.

Step into my embrace and you will find it

there.

## The Effect

A caress.

A kiss.

Sensuality pouring forth.

Like I've never known.

I'm fighting to keep the walls from falling.

You penetrate.

I realize that I cannot escape the feeling that is

overwhelming me.

I look into your eyes and become lost in the

deep

pools of brown.

My body opens up to you.

Comes alive.

Thriving on the skill of your hands, lips, tongue.

Is this really happening to me?

A stranger.

Connecting with the metaphysical me.

Not just the physical act of the climax.

But the sensual experience.

The intimate moments that makes it clear

that

I am present and not just getting mine.

I pull you closer.

No concept of time

or that this fantasy will end.

I inhale your scent deeply.

The feel of your skin.

The taste.

Never again will I accept the nonchalant

thrust of another body into mine.

I have been awakened by

A caress.

A kiss.

Sensuality pouring forth.

## QUANDARY

I want to let go and be me.

Not care if I look silly or vulnerable.

I look into your eyes and know that it would

be okay.

But I'm struggling to trust you.

You haven't given me pipe dreams or made

my hopes soar.

Still, I cannot completely live in the moment.

I am holding onto this last place in my heart

reserved for true love.

How do I tell you this?

Will you think that I am cynical?

Or that I want you to dwell in that place?

Even with all of the hesitation I feel I know

inexplicably that this experience is a part of

my destiny.

There is no "next lifetime".

I'm taking a step outside of what I can control.

Even if tears fall.

You don't call.

I act a fool.

Or things remain cool.

I am open to all that comes with knowing you

and you knowing me.

## SWEET WEAKNESS

Tell me what it is about me that makes you

weak?

Could it be the sensual curve of my hips?

Or the sweet roundness of my breasts that

lure you away

From the ordinary thoughts that become

consumed with

The nectar, sweet juices only I produce?

No fruit compares to the satisfaction I bring

after you have tasted

The fullness of my flavor.

Legs shaped delicately to encase the treasure

within.

That drives you to make promises just to smell

the aroma of- me.

A signature scent that lingers in the air with

each thought of

my walk, my smile.

The rhythm of my stride, the fullness of my

smile are evidence of the

Victory when the treasure is found.

# CAN I?

Can I come over and rub your shoulders?

Kiss your neck?

Let you know I missed you today.

Couldn't wait to see you so I could show you

all the ways this woman adores you.

I've drawn a hot bath for you.

Can I join you?

I want you to lie back on my chest and enjoy

the soothing heat of the water.

As I wrap my legs around you,

I lather your body

And whisper how I've yearned for your touch

I'm overcome with the need to have you

But I wait...this is my gift to you.

I want to pamper you and shower you with

love.

I want to envelope you in the security of my

heart.

I want you to know you're safe there.

Can I make love to you so sweet you can

barely breathe?

Can I call out your name and know you're

mine?

Can you reach out to me and feel this

connection?

We can make it simple.

Can I rub your shoulders and kiss your neck?...

## TRUTH

Remember the things I say to you

That will probably never be repeated.

When you kiss me, touch me, make love to me,

When my guard is totally down,

And I'm focused totally on the feelings, the

mood, the moments with you.

I am who I truly am.

Caught up in the mystery of our connection.

Absorbed in finding the core of what makes

you want me so passionately.

My words flow easily, uninhibited into your

ears

Allowing you access into my heart before the

moment ends and I am my guarded self again.

# I AM CERTAIN

With the dawning of each day.

When the Creator touches my heart and

I awaken.

I reach for you.

To feel the softness of your skin.

The texture of your hair.

I am certain I love you so completely.

I do not know where I begin and you end.

With each smile you give.

My heart grows with love for you.

I am joyful.

I embrace you.

To envelop you in the unconditional love that

pours from me.

I am certain I do not want to face a day

without you.

You are my precious gift.

My forever love.

With every "I love you" we exchange.

I know my purpose.

To never have you doubt.

You are my perfect fit.

I am mesmerized by your beauty and grace.

I am certain you were made for me and I for

you.

Through difficulties and triumphs.

We are destined to live this life together.

# EVERY PART OF YOU

There's no doubt my heart paces its beat with

yours.

Every part of you I love completely.

No conditions.

I am here for you with all the love I have.

You are my soul mate.

My dream come true.

Every part of you

Was made for me and me for you.

Through every trial we stand firm on the

promises of God.

Every victory we celebrate and give thanks to

the Almighty

For seeing us through.

For giving us to each other.

There's no doubt I breathe and am refreshed

by the joy of our love.

Every part of you I love completely.

No rhyme or reason.

I am blissfully, unchangeably in love with you.

You are my lover.

My strong shoulder.

Every part of you

Was made for me and me for you.

We will face challenges with unmovable faith.

We will continue to give thanks when the way

is smooth.

We are blessed to share this covenant.

Imperfect yet perfect for each other.

There's no doubt that I have waited for this

day, this moment.

Every part of you I love completely.

I belong to you.

My prayers have been answered to find my

once in a lifetime love.

You are my sweet passion.

Satisfying my every desire.

Every part of you

Was made for me and me for you.

We are assured of a blessing on our union

through our obedience to God.

We will keep Him at the center of our lives,

our marriage.

Thankful that we endured every test.

To arrive to this day to yes to our eternal love.

# IN LOVE WITH YOU

I am falling in love with you.

I've always loved you.

A lifetime.

Nothing changes it.

But...

This time falling in love with you is sunshine at

dawn.

The cooling of a sudden rain shower on a hot

day.

Sensual, soothing

Unexpected.

I am recapturing, rekindling the connection

we share.

A look, a smile, a touch.

Pure, genuine, soothing.

Falling, falling

Dizzying, mind altering

Love.

Every part of you is beautiful to me.

The soulful depths of your eyes.

The luscious curve of your lips.

Your stride.

Can't lie.

I am caught up.

In your sweet seduction.

My heart is singing a wonderful love song.

I am falling in love with you.

## THAT MAN

His hands are a balm to my soul.

A soother, a tender caresser.

Oh the touch of this man.

The look of this man.

The taste of this beautiful black man.

I could inhale the scent of his arousal.

The heat of his love every day.

Filling my body with sweet comfort.

Erotic sensations

It's just soooo,  oooh

Again and again

Over and over

The joy of our union

Higher and higher

Deeper and deeper

His presence is a balm to my soul

His quiet spirit makes me lose all control.

# CHOCOLATE

**Chocolate**

Sweet, smooth taste of chocolate

A delectable treat to your tongue.

Makes you hum

Come baby come...

Over here.

Share that **chocolate**.

Don't be shy.

My, My

Smooth **chocolate**.

Umm...

Lick the chocolate off or eat it all at once.

Nothing satisfies a craving like...

**Chocolate...**

Easy going down.

Heats you on a cold day.

Keeps the blues at bay.

Lingers on your finger tips.

The memory of putting your lips on the warm

tip of...

**Chocolate.**

Sweet, smooth taste.

**FALLING IN LOVE**

If I am falling in love,

let it be a soft landing into your arms

where I can feel your heart beating

and know although you may never say the

words,

I can feel it in the rhythm of our movements.

I don't want to consume your life.

Just share what I feel bursting out.

I don't want to miss the opportunity to know

you, to love you.

Doubt is powerful.

But I won't miss out on loving you.

If I am falling in love,

Let my heart always feel this joy.

# BELIEVE

Will you talk to me and tell me what matters

to you?

Will you trust me enough to let me in your

heart?

I just want a special corner where we can curl

up and

bring comfort and joy to each other.

Will you believe that I only want what you're

willing to give?

That although I care more each day,

I won't pressure you to give more.

I savor each moment when you reveal more

with a

touch or a look.

I will talk to you and tell what matters.

Be true to us and what is happening.

Even it's not what we hope.

Let's make it beautiful and forever a wonderful

experience.

## YOU KNOW THIS

I love you boy.

You get me and I get you.

You know this

Connection is unbreakable.

We join.

We separate.

But navigate right back to each other.

I love you boy.

That goofy smile that I adore.

The way you make me laugh like no one else

can.

I get you and you get me.

A bond that has remained since the first kiss.

We can never forget.

But we try.

We see each other smile and kiss.

It begins again.

I love you boy.

My heart wraps around yours.

You're always in my thoughts.

Time is of no importance.

Each time I see you.

I remember.

You get me and I get you.

I love you boy.

And you know this.

# LOVE

Romantic love is a beautiful, wondrous thing.

It's only when it is not the love meant for you

that the beauty dwindles in the copious tears

that are shed with this revelation.

The high of new love is an intoxication that is

heady and sweet.

A lethal combination when one needs to have

all senses keen to the truth–

This is not your love.

This is the love that you wanted so desperately

you accepted it any way it came.

Minimized you to maximize the hope that this

was finally it.

The great love that so many write about, sing

about.

Oh, but lamenting your foolishness for loving

out of turn does not turn back the hands of

time or the moments of passion that felt so

much like requited love.

It simply embitters and hardens your heart so

that your love,

The love that you believe God promised you

goes unfulfilled.

Love lessons are ongoing.

It is hit or miss.

Hopefully the numerous misses will result in

the one hit that will make your heart sing and

your spirits soar.

But, do not become so engrossed in keeping

your heart broken that when the true healing

touch of the Creator lifts you up, you miss the

gift He has promised.

Love is the greatest gift of all.

He would never deny you that.

Wait.

Be patient.

Be watchful.

Love whispers in your ear everyday its beauty.

# LET YOU IN

I took a chance and loved not only you but the

beauty of love.

I paused.

Inhaled.

Then slowly exhaled.

I had changed outwardly but the

transformation was evident.

Although I am still haunted by thoughts that I

will be heartbroken,

I am not consumed with building walls and

maintaining

boundaries.

Nor do I over analyze every syllable that exits

your mouth.

My instincts scream that I can trust you.

My heart longs to let you in.

My mind still treads cautiously.

In so many ways I know you well while not

really knowing

you at all.

Questions remain unspoken and unanswered.

I do not want to disturb the comfortable

compatibility of

our relationship.

At this moment I am happy with what is

happening.

That love is in the air.

That we're not tripping and falling in.

Taking the time to savor the beauty of love is

healing.

Even when the physicality of love ends the

true intent will survive.

I've always loved you.

I am grateful to experience this beauty with

you in this season of my life.

I will not trespass or take this experience for

granted.

## NOT A FOREVER SITUATION

It feels real in your arms.

Settle down comfort of true love.

Connected like electricity to a power switch.

Vibe magnetic

Kinetic energy explosive

Deep in my bones feelings

That move me to come back to you again.


Temporary yet genuine emotions

That make us stare into each other's eyes

Touch, caress, taste, feel to make certain it

Is not an apparition

A fleeting ghost with the power to make

climatic

Surges turn us inside out!

It's not a forever situation.

Temporary equation that sums up to you

going into me,

Me dividing you between two...

Willing the clock to stop on this moment

Frozen in time

Where this is a forever situation.

## HEART HEALING EXPERIENCE

Take a chance and let life heal what is broken.

Let the unexpected guide you to the healing

springs.

Don't miss your heart healing experience by

fearing what

Others may think.

Their thoughts have stalled their journeys

Keep your head up and your heart open.

Love is in the moments that do not

immediately capture

Your attention.

A tender cheek caress.

A hello beautiful.

Healing words from an unlikely source.

A person you would normally dismiss because

of packaging.

Because your perception has altered your

reality.

A heart healing experience will reintroduce you

to the life you deserve.

Prepare you for the love designed for you.

Generate joy

Permeate your core with hope

Elevate your thinking to demand more than

the ordinary.

Break down barriers to live free and in living

color!

Healed!

# WONDERFUL ENCOUNTER

It's not often I meet a man whose mere touch

can turn my body on and

Make it melt into sweet submission.

All I want is the slightest touch of his lips on

my neck,

His hands gently caressing my back.

His voice beckoning me to places of pleasure so

exquisite

I tremble in his arms.

This man whose charm is so disarming.

Disposition so unimposing.

Just mild, somewhat meek.

Then like a lightning bolt he strokes the very

essence

Of my femininity.

I know I am a woman 210%.

Strong, black, powerful, fearfully and

wonderfully made.

But... I am transported within myself to a

place where

I connect and love again.

Where I'm not encased in this hard exterior I

carefully

Construct each day.

I am able to accept what I deserve –

The tender affection and devoted attention of

this man.

Savoring every moment before the ultimate

union of our bodies.

I am not embarrassed to say that the

experience leaves me

Quivering hours later.

Each memory quickens my pulse.

Shortens my breath.

Effectively, succinctly and articulately said,

The man makes my toes curl.

My mouth water.

He knows the spot without a doubt.

He is my chocolate fix.

The ultimate _____!

He has the love I dig.

This poetic prose is beautiful but I want to be

real and you

How I feel.

He touches ME, not just this body.

Perfecting the chance between a man and a

woman

That started at the beginning of time

Taking this woman gently in his arms,

Shielding me from me,

I am thankful for this wonderful encounter.

## WHY

You ask why you haven't heard my voice.

I have been talking to you in my heart.

In my thoughts.

I am constantly in touch with your energy.

Hoping you can feel the waves as they travel

to where you are.

Listen carefully when the birds sing.

The wind blows.

When you feel the sun on your face.

You can hear my voice.

I am telling you I love you.

I am concerned about you.

I am happy for you.

I am praying for you.

You ask why you haven't heard my voice.

I place your hand on your heart.

Listen to your heartbeat.

When you think of me I am there.

I poured my love into your being.

I won't leave.

I cannot leave.

When you close your eyes and you hear a faint

whisper that is reminiscent of me,

Be still and listen carefully.

I am sending peace, joy and love to you.

You ask why you haven't heard my voice.

I simply smile and say

Simply connect with who you know I am.

You will hear my voice.

# REAL

I am not a fantasy.

Long, Nubian legs that open wide enticing

your strong lean body to join me in the most

fantastic journey your mind can imagine but

your body can barely handle.

Breasts that nourish you.

A suckle so sweet you lick your lips from the

memory.

An ass round and firm, built to satisfy you

only as a Black woman could.

However, I am not a fantasy.

I am real, can you deal?

Intelligent, well spoken, gentle, firm.

Will you learn?

I am your past, present and future.

Not an afterthought, but a part of what we

can be and I have determined shall be.

I am not fantasy.

I am that sugar that makes your coffee sweet.

That driving bass in every beat.

The heat from a bath that soothes you.

The moan in jazz that moves you.

I am that cool drink of water that quenches

you when the sweat from your body drips...

After my long, Nubian legs entice you to places

only imagined but you now know are real.

Can you deal?

# THE EXPOSÈ OF A QUESTION

Do you love me? OR

Do you only love the way my hands caress

your body when

I wantonly ask you for more?

Hands that become nails passionately raking

your skin when I...

Do you love me? OR

Just the sway of my hips when I see you in a

crowd?

Hips that fit into yours so smoothly when we

dance to a slow jam...

Do you love me? OR

Just the way I call you Daddy when the only

light is the flicker of

A candle?

When I say you're the man, the only man.

Come get me.

Satiate me...

Hmmm...

Do I love you?

Well, I love that God made a man who can

give me more,

Sustain a little pain...

Turn a set of hips into a well-oiled machine.

Be my man and handle his baby's needs.

It's time to start again? (Smiling)

Do you love me?

## SWEET WEAKNESS

Tell me what it is about me that makes you

weak?

Could it be the sensual curve of my hips?

Or the sweet roundness of my breasts that

lure you away

From the ordinary thoughts that become

consumed with

The nectar, sweet juices only I produce?

No fruit compares to the satisfaction I bring

after you have tasted

The fullness of my flavor.

Legs shaped delicately to encase the treasure

within.

That drives you to make promises just to smell

the aroma of- me.

A signature scent that lingers in the air with

each thought of

my walk, my smile.

The rhythm of my stride, the fullness of my

smile are evidence of the

Victory when the treasure is found.

## YOU

Believing in the power of this connection that

is all about

You

A constant, powerful vibe that holds my love

deep inside.

Unable to truly release what only you increase

with the mere

Touch of fingertips.

Only you can ignite, excite, satisfy, magnify,

titillate, stimulate, copulate

As fulfill this longing that is deep and

everlasting.

A meeting of minds that defies time

Shivers down my spine.

The memories so divine.


Your words so true.

What would I do if I had never met you?

A meeting of two souls taking hold of stories

untold, bold.


Creating fire, desire on the verge of release

Sweet, sweet peace

Believing in the power of this connection that

is all about you.

I opened for my beloved, but my beloved had left; he was gone. My heart sank at his departure. I looked for him but did not find him. I called him but he did not answer. Song of Solomon 5:6

## CRAZY BITCH

You convince yourself that I am a crazy bitch.

A disenchanted, man hating damaged

Bitch

You take no responsibility for your narcissistic

borderline psychotic contribution to this

rollercoaster I did not buy a ticket to ride.

You say "that bitch is hot and cold.  She is a

bipolar, fucked up in the head piece of work.  I

was trying to work with her.  Show her the

kindness of real man.  Hell, that bitch is

tripping."

It doesn't matter that you were only

concerned about your gratification.

What was in it for you.

Selfishness is your moral compass.

You get yours and if there are crumbs, maybe

I could scoop those ups.

You know, I agree.

I am a crazy bitch.

Crazy to give you my time.

Share my world.

Feed your carnal and basic needs.

Crazy to give you my heart.

Let you into the depths of my soul.

Tell you my hopes, dreams and secrets.

But what is your excuse for being the non-

factor, sorry excuse of a man you are?

Illusions of grandeur fill your conversations.

I stood by your silly ass.

Supporting your dreams.

Encouraging your "ambitions".

Crazy bitch?

Coming from you, those words hold no power.

They do not alter the course of my life.

Your hatred I simply devour.

Regurgitate and feed back to you.

Expose you as the weak, pathetic man you are.

Left alone to be the only crazy bitch who was

in that scene.

## HERO WORSHIPER

I am not an ordinary woman.

Not by far.

I am more than capable of taking care of

myself.

Self-reliant.

Sexy.

Absolutely irresistible.

Intelligent.

Outspoken.

A catch.

A solid sister who holds her man down.

My stronghold, my weakness is

I am a hero worshiper.

That might sound unusual, even weird to you.

When a man has made it evident he wants to

sample my honey.

I size him up to make sure he meets my

standards.

Tall, well-built, well-dressed, well-spoken,

well...

You know.

I don't want my cookie stirred if the spoon is

not large enough.

If all the wells are met, I become so enthralled

in the experience of being with this man.

The hero worshiping begins.

No one can tell me a thing about my boo.

I make sure his wells are kept up.

I don't let him out of my sight!

I keep and maintain his superman shirt and

cape.

My worship is so out of control I fail to notice

that I've never been to his home, met his

friends, know where he works...

What the hell?

He's getting mail at my house?

I am always spotting him $20 for gas.

Paying for a night out.

Just when I am ready to put his ass out,

He brings the best part of his hero,

I fall down on my knees and worship.

Sing at the top of my voice when he turns me

out, in, upside down, right-side up!

I am a hero worshiper.

I can't deny it.

Wouldn't even try.

But heroes are made to be replaced.

I'm on the lookout for Captain Can't Get

Enough!

# THANK YOU

I want to thank you for treating me like shit.

I want to thank you for the mental kicks,

punches and back hand slaps.

I want to thank you for the perfect execution

of a plan to destroy my self-esteem and self-

worth.

I want to thank you for giving me a Cinderalla

complex when you recounted the wonderful

times you had out with your friends.

Thank you for treating me with total

disregard in public.

Relegating me to the status of the chic you

fucked but was not your girlfriend.

Thank you for telling me how socially inept

and awkward I was.

Thank you for turning every conversation into

a lecture of why I was wrong.

Thank you for objectifying me and making me

your freak, your whore.

Thank you for calling me crazy.

Thank you for the bitter, acrid taste of my

tears.

The heart wrenching pain of rejection.

I cannot thank you enough for being the

egotistical asshole you are.

You are true to that and have no desire to

change.

You believe your hype.

Thank you because I now realize I was the best

thing that ever entered your world.

Thank you for not making me your girl.

Thank you for not associating yourself with me.

It's the best rejection you gave me.

Thank you for not introducing me to your

friends.

Not including me in your imaginary circle of

influence.

Thank you for casting me away.

You gave me my freedom.

Thank you for showing me who you really

were 100% of the time.

Thank you for setting the example of what I

do not want.

Thank you for forcing self-evaluation.

Thank you for never considering my feelings.

I would have continued to believe that all you

needed was time.

You would see that I was the best thing that

ever happened to you.

Thank you for shaking me to the core.

I would have never gotten me back.

## MY HEART

I presented to you my heart.

Pure and genuine.

Filled with love.

Overflowing.

You took my heart and promptly stood on it.

No regard to the pain you caused.

No notice of the tears that flowed down my

face.

I kept holding on to you.

Never realizing you were not holding me too.

I was embracing your back.

Sometimes hanging on precariously.

Being dragged through life by you.

Emotionally battered and scarred.

I was oblivious to the pain.

I presented to you my heart.

It was all had I left.

I abandoned my dignity.

There was no self-love.

Time spent waiting for you to make my heart

beat again.

Chasing you through a never ending maze of

valleys.

No peaks.


I kept holding on to you.

Giving you life.

Mistaking the throb of your dick as your

heartbeat.

The swell of my clit as love.

You languished in my hot, liquid canal.

Taking everything I offered selfishly.

I presented to you my heart.

My goddamn heart!

You placed it your hand and squeezed the joy,

the love and the hope out of it.

I looked at myself, not you, and saw the truth.

You did not ask for my heart.

So it held no value.


I no longer hold on to you.

I embrace myself.

Loving who I am.

# SWEET TALKER

**Such a sweet talker.**

Panty dropping words for the chic who thrives

on flowery language.

But for the chic who's heard it all...

entertainment.

Takes more than sweet words to convince me

that you deserve the goodness I have.

The words slide from your tongue.

The delicious sounds flow from your mouth.

The goal is to have me supine, prone,

horizontal, vertical

It really doesn't matter how you get it as long

as it's got!

Such a sweet talker.

Sugar drips from your tongue like honey from

a comb.

Afraid of being alone and faced with the

words that flow like water from your mouth.

Lies that burn your throat and assault your

nostrils with the stench.

The words are empty even to your ears.

The truth of your deception pushed into the

recesses of your soul where a conscience no

longer resides.

A magnetic force pulls you to the female scent.

Reminisce does not satisfy.

You must know this one as well.

Such a sweet talker.

Words used as a backdrop for a life that's a

fantasy.

Hiding who you really are.

Robbing me of the opportunity to hear the

truth, your truth.

In your past is the one who spoke sweet

nothings to you.

Teaching you that genuine hearts are made to

be broken.

Disposable emotions that you have no

attachments.

Hollow echoes of your sweet words resonate in

the minds of those who believed you when the

words slid from your tongue.

Such a sweet talker.

Bordering on the ridiculous.

Pontifications disguised as romance.

Putting the unsuspecting in a trance.

Hearing words that have no meaning.

Just empty sounds covering up the

Saccharine laced utterances of the sweet

talker.

Never giving up his quest to cover you in the

Stickiness of his jive.

## DAWN'S SONG

I've heard it said that joy comes in the

morning.

The dawn is the awakening of the day.

Well, my dawn song is one of lamentation.

Tear stained pillows.

My joy is you.

You're gone.

My joy went with you.

The midnight hour does not deliver me from

my anguish.

Another lie I was told.

I sing my dawn song every day.

Hoping that you will hear it and realize I am

incomplete without you.

I dream of your return,

Your apologetic words.

Your concern for my heart that you have

broken into a million pieces.

Many say no one can steal my joy.

They are right.

I freely gave you my joy.

You were in control.

I believed that made you happy.

You have composed this dawn song.

I am tired of singing it.

The tears are futile.

My heart still hurts but I feel a little joy

warming it with the love I have for myself.

My dawn song was drowning out my self-

worth.

I have a new song.

And it's not about the joy that left but the

rebirth of the joy I could not give away.

# THE TRUTH

Talk to me, the truth only.

Not words to stir my emotions and make me

dream,

Believe that you treasure me, want me in your

life.

Hearts connected by love.

Bodies quivering from climaxes that defy

reason.

Dreaming about giving you the sweet, sweet

juices that flow from a glance.

Entranced, mesmerized.

All for you.


I need you to do the unusual.

Admit the truth.

You are not the man I need.

You do not treasure me, but love the control

you have over my emotions.

Giving me hope, then snatching it away.

Listen to me!

Hear the truth!

My heart is paced by your actions.

You lie to me.

It breaks.

You ignore me.

It dies.

No more giving unselfishly to a man who is

incapable of recognizing strength personified.

Beauty magnified.

A woman, transparent, in love with a lie...

What appears to be love but is a tragic

reflection of who she is inside.

Insecure, unsure, accepting a man incapable of

loving her, himself, life.

## MEANTIME

It embarrasses me to admit that I cannot give

an audible voice to the insecurities I feel about

you.

I love you.

I love being with you anywhere.

Yet, it's as though whatever this is we're doing

happens in a parallel or alternate universe.

I listened carefully to you when you were

annoyed with me that day.

Became more aware of how I treated you and

our friendship.

I realized I wanted a relationship with you

that would be more than "friends with

benefits".

That has never worked for me when it came

to you.

Am I still missing the mark?

Or was it too little too late on my part when I

started including you in my plans and spent

more time with you?

It seems that things have flipped.

I want to be with you and do the things you

enjoy.

Meet the people in your life.

But, you're not including me.

When you mention me, who do you say I am?

When I mention you, I say you're my

sweetheart, my honey bunch.

I am not beat for a title.

I'm just feeling like someone you're cool with

but no one should know about.

I want to ask you, how can you go places

without me?

But the words are stuck in my throat.

I don't want to be demanding.

I'm afraid what I think is the truth.

Or you just haven't given any thought to

inviting me to listen to jazz, to a play or

whatever.

I'm hurt every time you recount an event.

I cry like a 16 year old when I feel rejected.

Still I eagerly experience your life vicariously.

I wait until you want to be with me.

I make myself available so you will know I

want to be with you.

I try so, so hard to just accept it and not

make waves.

Just live my life the way I always have and

not dwell on what's bothering me.

I want complete honesty from you.

I need it.

Is this an in the meantime situation?

## THE PAIN

Living, I was told, was done abundantly,

With abandon.

Like it was your last day on earth.

For me, happiness was fleeting,

Joy was elusive.

Revisiting the pain, was a connection to

breathing.

Pain evoked emotions,

Tears, anger, frustration.

The pain kept my blood flowing,

My lungs functioning.

Pain was familiar, strangely comforting.

I knew it well.

We were lovers, strange bedfellows.

Hating each other, but unable to leave the

dysfunction,

Of a love so strong...

I was able to wear a smile that belied the

troubles,

The storms that brewed.

The turmoil that grew deep in my belly.

A labor that I knew was inevitable.

When would the eruption of this birth occur?

The offspring would be the hideous spawn of

my fears, insecurities, shame.

In the moment I thought I would not breathe

again.

When the pain no longer felt familiar, brought

comfort.

Life, the sweet, surreal feeling

Grabbed hold of my lungs and pushed out a

force of air.

Compelling me to open my eyes to the truth.

The pain, certainly a part of me, had become

an addiction.

Blocking my destiny.

Controlling my thoughts.

Stealing my dreams.

Living, I am doing it abundantly, with

abandon, making my mark.

# FINESEXYCHOCOLATEASS

All of this in one man?

Surely you can understand why I made

**finesexychocolateass** one word.

All be told.

It's sure to unfold that I could not resist the

combination in

This man.

I could not stand

This specimen made the demand that I recline

While he dined

And I languished in the pleasure that this

treasure

So skillfully provided.

Can't deny it

I was ready, willing and able to reciprocate

Duplicate

The pleasure I received

On my knees

If it pleased

Him.

All the way to my chin

I'm hooked!

Shooked

Up by his presence

Pure decadence

All of this in one man!

His **finesexychocolateass**

Has my nose wide open

As well as my legs

My mouth begs for the sweet release

Please, please!

Fine   Sexy   Chocolate   Ass

Give me what I need

Is what I plead.

Ah!  Damn!

Hits the spot every time...

# ORGASMIC SOULMATE

## Orgasm

The desired end to a sexual encounter.

The apex of sexual stimulation with a partner

or solo.

A feeling of euphoria.

Glorious pleasure.

Delicious.

My orgasmic soul mate is not limited to fine

tuning my

body and producing Richter scale climaxes.

He is the one who connects with me

metaphysically.

He anticipates my wants, my needs.

With a glance he can gauge my mood.

My orgasmic soul mate nurtures harmony in

our relationship.

Discord is like nails on a chalkboard.

He rejects negativity.

Focusing instead on the joys and pleasures of

life.

Connecting with me on intellectual levels that

produce mind

altering physical connections.

A man strong, virile, assured.

Deep brown eyes that look into my soul.

Eyes that are able to see my heartbeat.

His fingertips are on the pulse of what drives

me.

Fills me with the energy to go after and

achieve goals.

My orgasmic soul mate climaxes with me.

He waits for the signal that I am ready to

explode in his arms.

Guiding me back to reality.

Whispering that we're not done but only just

begun to take

on the world

And yell out in satisfaction one orgasm at a

time.

## WE SAY

We say, "I love you" then make love.

This is love to us.

The connection of our bodies.

The heat, the passion

No longer sharing words,

Embraces, kisses

Just making love

'Cause this is love in action

No form, no structure

No heart

You connect with me

But the disconnect is evident.

Your time with me is spent trying to achieve

the ultimate orgasm.

Sweat, loins moving at a frantic pace to expel

what your body

cannot hold.

Wasted seed, unrealized joy of love.

On the sheets, floor, me.

My time with you is spent trying to bridge the

disconnect.

The obvious quest to get a semblance of love.

An act that can be done alone.

The result the same

Wasted seed, unrealized joy of love

No tender look, embrace

No words of desire, adoration.

I place one hand over your heart feeling the

beat return

to steady.

You immediately disconnect, move away

Love is over.

It is not spoken of again.

I wonder if you say "I love you" to her

Then make love

No form, no structure

Or do you instead hold her close, lovingly

No wasted seed, but realized joy of love.

## NO NAME NEEDED

**No name needed.**

He knows who he is.

I know he's in the room without seeing his face.

My body is tune to his scent, his swagger.

I feel his breath on my neck as he approaches.

**No name need.**

He knows who he is.

He isn't my man

Not any more

But, once we shared passion unbridled.

Now we're linked by sexual energy that's like

a hang man's noose.

I want to walk away and not look back.

But this feeling begins in my toes.

**No name needed.**

He knows who he is.

Constantly trying to be in his space

But he limits my time in his presence

Making me want to do more than the other

chic.

Just to see him all the time, any time.

**No name needed.**

He knows who he is.

It's more than a shame that I find myself

again wanting

this man.

He so evidently doesn't want me.

I accept his invitations for light banter and

fuck sessions.

Anyway I can have him,

I allow that shit to happen.

**No name needed.**

He knows who he is.

The humiliation of my anonymity is a painful

reminder

that my name is forgotten.

He doesn't care who I am.

**No name needed.**

# TEARS ON MY PILLOW

Someone touches my back, my neck, my face

He leans in close.

I smile with my eyes closed.

I sit up quickly.

"What are you doing here?"

"I used my key," he says and smiles.

"I still have access."

"I am too careless with my shit!" I think to

myself.

"I hope that's not a problem."

He moves familiarly around my bedroom.

The room is dim.

Only the light from several candles illuminate

the room.

He sits casually on my bed.

His hand touches my pillow.

"There are tears on your pillow.  Let me make

it better.

I can make you smile."

The sheet begins to slide.

He is aroused.

He leans in to kiss me fully on the mouth.

Suddenly inhaling the scent.

The heat of the bodies that were earlier

entwined.

He takes a step back.

Seeing on my face satiation, a glow.

"No, these are not tears on my pillow..."

# ODE TO LOVE LOST

Without hesitation I loved every part of you.

No conditions.

I accepted you as you were.

I was concerned about what mattered to you.

All I wanted to do was love you.

I was transparent and open.

Ready to give all that I had.

You chose parts of me to love.

When your choices were made, I didn't have

much to offer.

There were conditions.

Hurtful words full of criticism.

I was your secret.

No open show of affection for the woman who

dropped everything to take care of your needs.

I lost parts of me.

Neglected parts of me.

Hated parts of me.

I believed your distorted view of me.

Shared you with the ghosts of girlfriends past.

I could not win.

In your memory, they were womanhood

personified.

Their perfection overrode the pain they caused.


I love every part of you.

Everything.

Absolutely everything.

But not enough to let you kill my spirit.

Things that make me me.

My quiet nature.

My rambling conversation.

The extra weight.

The joy I find in being alone.

I love every part of me.

Everything.

Absolutely everything.

## SLICK

You try to convince me that the slick shit you

present is concern about

Your welfare and mine.

I doubt you're concerned about me.

You believe the hype about yourself that you

intake like vitamins.

This chauvinistic bullshit that you are pure and

untainted by the vaginas

You have sucked, fucked and tucked- in.

I can't imagine the level of absurdity you live.

The mindset that you adopted to justify the

whore you really are.

keeping women under your feet.

Firmly.

So much that they believe your shit don't stink

and that your body

has been spared from the ills of life.

Your words are heard but unlike the sex we

had they did not penetrate.

Each sexy, nasty moment we shared you gave

every ounce of who you were

While my pretty, pink vagina pushed back on

your sheets that have seen the

asses of many.

Only I leave whole, not broken, by your

twisted words.

# ENDURE

I endure the pain of accepting that I will be

alone.

Brief lust affairs that frustrate and further

harden my heart.

What is love?

It seems to squirt out with each ejaculation.

Making a mess inside and outside my body.

Soiling sheets

Washed away by the scrub of the machine.

Yet leaving behind the mess that I mistakenly

thought

was genuine affection.

Only injecting my heart with regret, rejection

Possibly corroding the vital vessel that allows

blood flow to vital organs.

I feel myself changing.

Becoming robotic in my approach.

Eating and drinking simply to remain vital.

Thinking only professionally, academically

Turning off love to those not familial

In my mind I am alone.

Grasping to the wisp of sanity that keeps me

among

the definitively sane.

I long to languish in the truth of who I am.

Simply a woman who has tried love over and

over

but always accepts that love is evasive and

duplicitous.

# WHAT MATTERS

Have you ever realized that what you thought

mattered was actually taking up too much of

your brain matter?

You spend great amounts of energy pondering

and pondering over a situation that did not

deserve any of your precious time?

Or people who did not care if you ever

breathed again?

Precious minutes lost to fruitless endeavors.

How can I help them?

How can I resolve this?

Why don't they like me?

Why am I excluded?

Stop...

Take that energy and put it into more

rewarding efforts.

Strengthening your spiritual walk.

Strengthening your body.

Strengthening your mind.

Until you realize that trying to complete

yourself with people who do not have it

together any more than you, your mind will

remain a battle ground.

Your heart will always be broken.

The void will remain.

The stuff, things will pile up and you will

wonder why in the hell do I have all of this

SHIT?!

Your options?

Press your diaphragm and blow out as hard as

you can ALL of the toxins.

Negative energies, thoughts of inadequacy,

self-doubt, low self-esteem, poor self-image.

Then inhale deeply with your face raised to

Heaven believing that all that was promised to

you will permeate, saturate your being.

Trusting that what God has for you is for you.

Let the haters hate.

Give them something to emulate but never

duplicate.

You are an original.

Let your walk speak for you.

Let your talk only give blessings.

The things that matter will not keep you up at

night or beleaguer your mind.

You will find peace in slumber.

The things that don't matter will never enter

your mind.

Your realizations will be about things that have

a purpose.

# CAN'T

I can't do this anymore.

I've tried.

Rearranged my life, who I am.

Given myself to this second chance

but this is not for me.

I'm frustrated by the complicated spin on life

that you've given me.

The imperfections of my life are missed.

Idiosyncrasies that identified me as an

individual.

Not this bullshit ride that you refuse to stop

and let me off.

Apathetic and frustrated that I've given you

control of

my life.

Trying to fulfill your desire to have and to

hold.

Truth be told

Vows would be shallow, superficial

I can't do this anymore.

I've tried and tried to this your way

Only to lose my way through my life's journey.

I WON'T do this anymore.

I don't want to try.

I'm taking back my power that I so freely gave

you

And you misused.

The cycle ends here.

# FALLING

If love is the greatest gift, why do we fall in it?

Falling creates a crisis.

We do everything we can to break the fall.

Is that why hearts sometimes break?

We try to cushion the fall.

Is that why we sometimes tell white lies?

Love is supposed to surround, envelope.

Why then do we express so much happiness

when we fall in?

Once we're there then what?

Are we constantly trying to climb out, fall

deeper,

become buried?

I am not opposed to love, more specifically,

romantic love.

Nor am I in the middle.

I hope one day we will stand in love.

Upright, fully cognizant of what is happening.

Not falling and concentrating on what

happens when we land softly or hard.

but standing in who we were before love

arrived.

Not constantly seeking approval because the

fall happened

separately from our partner.

But standing confidently, purposely, strong,

vibrant.

See, when we stand in love we are gazing eye

to eye with our beloved.

Not searching for our  beloved as we fall

hoping we're not alone.

Are you able to stand in love?

Or do you believe the only way to love is while

falling, reaching,

grasping for something strong to steady you?

Stand for something or you'll fall for anything.

# I LIKE YOU

I listen to your heartbeat.

I feel your body's heat.

I move closer to receive your forehead kiss.

You whisper, "I like you."

A lump forms in my throat.

I like you too.

I like the way you look at me.

I like when you take my hand to lead me to

your bedroom

I like the way you take control.

Bringing me pleasure again and again.

I like the unbridled passion that pours from us

like hot lava.

I like that there is no awkwardness between us.

I like that being me is a gift to you.

I could spend a lifetime in your arms kissing

you.

Enveloping you in the warmth of my heart

where true love dwells.

Yet, I hold back because I could love you so

completely, so totally.

Unhesitatingly giving you all the love your

heart could hold.

So I choose to like you instead.

Mutual fondness that won't break our hearts.

The thin line that allows me to feel love in

your presence

Without the pressure of the revelation that I

love you.

And the silence that follows when you hold me

close,

Give me a forehead kiss and say, "I like you."

# GOOD-BYE

Good-byes are difficult.

It is never easy to face the reality that you

may never see

a person again.

That no matter how well you connected,

you will not stay in touch.

However, the unspoken good-bye is like being

in a cocoon.

It wants to break free but cannot or will not.

A beautiful butterfly will not emerge.

Only the bittersweet memories of happy

moments.

As the time fast approached that you would

say good-bye

every excuse was given to avoid the moment.

Adding to your grief of sharing a hug, kiss or

whispered words,

you believed that not saying good-bye would

freeze time in the relationship.

Only now you realize that you are in a time

warp.

Unable to move past the regret of not saying

good-bye.

The fantasy that you created has made the

reality of your broken heart

more painful.

You tried to make the good-bye carefree and

light hearted.

Unable to accept the connection you felt.

You donned a take it or leave it coat of armor.

Now this good-bye, this unspoken good-bye,

has a grip around

your throat.

A vise so tight you cannot inhale or exhale.

You pray the fear of good-bye will not prevent

your from

accepting the love energy that waits to wrap

itself around you.

Possibly leading you to another good-bye.

Hug, kiss, say the words you mean.

Life is moments filled with beauty.

Within good-bye there are treasured moments

of passion, love,

and hope.

Remember, following closely behind a good –

bye is a hello.

# TIRED

I'm tired of the uncertainty.

The desire to please you.

Keep you interested.

It's chipping away my resolve.

The comfort I feel in my own skin.

I've only know this insecurity with you.

Am I smart enough?

Pretty enough?

Sophisticated enough?

Thin enough?

I lose myself in you anticipating your needs.

My heart breaks when you don't call.

When you do,

I run to you.

Heart, arms and legs wide open to receive the

remnants

of your affection.

Wanting to walk away but holding on to the

hope that you will see

the treasure I am.

Feeling foolish, abandoned and deceived does

not

diminish the high regard I hold you.

In my mind your acceptance of me is a mere

second away.

What I deserve is secondary

It should be simple for me to walk away and

never look

back.

But it seems we are never finished.

Always in each other's thoughts.

I think of you with love and forevers.

You think of me reminiscently and with

temporaries.

I'm tired of the uncertainty

The tears, the heartache

The ease that I let you have me.

Tired of the emptiness of loving you.

# APART

We were apart but I hadn't released you.

Each day I thought of you.

About your well-being, situation.

I could not remove you from my heart.

Without provocation I would think of how you

made

Me laugh loudly at your antics.

I hear music and remember the shared love.

I see your soulful eyes that I would become lost.

Longing to gain access to your innermost

thoughts.

Striving to take on your burdens.

Carry them until you were strong again.

I realized what was so difficult for me to

release was easy for you.

The emotional ties I bound myself with did not

encumber you.

The emotions I drowned in you floated on and

made

it to shore.

Dry land filled with opportunities.

Dark clouds loom in the distance.

Sunshine strived to shine on me to warm the

chill in my heart.

Deep in my soul I hear the fervent cry

"Release him! He is free.  You are the captive!"

Today it does not hurt to let go of the past.

The one love I believed unparalleled.

I never wanted to lose that feeling.

But it keeps me in a rut.

A vicious cycle that becomes more difficult

each time.

As I sever the soul tie I can hear the familiar

cry,

*"One more try."*

We are apart and I have released you.

I have freed myself from the self-imposed

prison of

we belong together.

# WEAK AND UNINSPIRED

Love is for the weak and uninspired.

Moans and groans of unrequited emotions

Produces apathetic souls that wonder aimlessly

from soul to soul

Forming ties that stretch into a noose

Choking joy and hope out of the hearts of

those

who were once joyously in love.

Love is for the weak and uninspired.

Energy draining joining of loins

frantically striving to climax

Only to crash with the realization that a

nut is not love.

Just an end to a means.

A wet ass and nine months of waiting for the

Promised seed to manifest love.

Love is for the weak and uninspired.

Trapped in a world of promises that are

broken like hearts.

The greatest gift treated like a dime store toy.

Disposable, expendable

Arrogantly looking you in the eyes demanding

your

Strong and inspired soul to surrender to the

destruction

and seduction of love.

## WANT FROM ME

I asked you what you wanted from me.

You replied, "Your last breath."

So that you would never have to hear my

voice again.

The questions that erupt like a volcano from

my mouth.

You could witness my demise and know I saw

the disdain in your eyes.

"My last breath is what you want?"  I asked.

"I would've easily given you that.

Even if it gave you pleasure.

I would rather give you all the love my heart

holds."

I said pitifully hoping love would conquer all.

Win him over so he would see my reason for

living was

to one day have his heart.

He looked me squarely in my eyes and said,

"Die bitch die!

You let a pity fuck turn you out.

Calling me all the time, sweating me

Listen, I am going to put you out of your

misery.

I don't want you!

Will never love you!

Cannot stand the sight of you!''

I looked at him.

Finally seeing the light.

I said, "My last breath is what you need to live.

I am not God so that you will not receive.

You want me to die?

The old me has met her demise

The new me has risen like a phoenix flying

high.

Soaring above your disdain.

It no longer matters what you want from

me."

# THE BATTLE

There is a battle going on between my head

and my heart.

Intellectually I can identify every reason I

should run not walk away

from the situation.

My heart wants to open up,

but I do not want to take a chance on the

pain and

brokenness that accompanies love.

You're a kind, gentle, peaceful soul with the

power to ignite

or extinguish these flames of love.

Of course, you're not responsible for my fear

to love.

You have never spoken an unkind word or

rejected my desire

to be in your presence.

But the battle intensifies and I feel the need to

run before

something tragic happens.

I search my memory for a time I was deeply

in love and

Believed it would last.

I cannot remember that time.

I've always been my biggest obstacle.

My worst enemy.

It is unfair to subject you to this uncertainty.

I try to mimic your carefree, nonchalance.

But my mind and my heart are not equipped

that way.

Hence, they battle and cause undue stress.

I finally give in.

Shut down and walk away.

Perhaps not from the greatest love of my life

but from

a chance to love and receive love on some level.

Will I ever win this battle?

Or do I need to wage war?

## LEARNING

Learning to live without you while still loving

you is ridiculous.

Yet each day it gets easier.

This scares me.

I don't want to know what it's like not to miss

you.

I believe deep within that ending this

attachment will save me from heartache.

Still I want to inhale your scent.

Kiss you deeply.

Make love to you uninhibitedly.

I feel you seeping out of my pores.

Your energy that has surrounded me is waning.

I taste the unshed tears.

I feel the shed tears on my cheeks.

Why is love so brief yet so poignant?

My passion lies at your feet waiting to be

embraced, caressed.

# NEVER MINE

How do I let go of what was never mine?

On borrowed time

Connecting and subjecting myself to emotions

that seemed real

But fleeting.

Reveling in the temporary joy of love.

Basking in the afterglow

Only to become an afterthought

Letting go of what I never held is a loss that is

hollow.

Echoes of whispered words

Expressions of wants and desires that were

unattainable.

How do I let of of what was never mine?

Flowing like wine

Tears of loss

I can hear your voice.

Feel your touch

I already miss your smile.

Your proclamations that I am amazing,

beautiful.

Another time perhaps we would be forever,

But right now I have to let go of what was

never mine.

# FREELY

I give myself permission to let the tears flow.

Freely.

It is the only way I can purge the grief that

strains my heart.

I miss your smile.

Your laugh.

Your stride.

I believed that we would stand the tests of

time.

An everlasting love.

Passion that linked us beyond space and time.

I think about you and being in your arms.

Bodies entangled.

Freely.

Touching you.

You touching me.

Perfection.

I love you and wanted you to love me.

I threw caution to the wind and released my

soul to you.

I give myself permission to forgive myself for

this misplaced love.

I forgive you for taking advantage of my

devotion.

Freely.

I open myself to the universe to receive my

healing.

To restore the joy in loving me.

To release the despair I feel in letting you go.

Returning you to find the energy that you

should connect.

Allowing me accept the love that I deserve.

From myself not another.

Freely.

I accept that I misjudged the connection we've

always shared.

Placing it in the past where it should dwell.

No longer mistaking it for soulmate love.

Our souls have changed.

They are strangers now.

Perhaps in another lifetime

Hello will be a welcomed sound.

For now

Freely

Goodbye

# SCREAM: KAT'S STORY

The scream fights daily to break free from the prison of decorum to which I sentenced it.   Oftentimes the break out is imminent at the most inopportune times; in the car, in the elevator, at my desk, at church. I hold it in.   No one can know that a breakdown not a breakthrough is in that gut wrenching scream that constantly threatens to break free from the clutches of my throat.

I say a breakdown because within that scream are years of hurts, disappointments and frustrations. The tears would be volcanic. So intense who I am would die. There's no guarantee that a new me would emerge.   A scream so intense even I could not be sure it would not scare me shitless.   Can you imagine living your life in constant fear that a scream will expose you as a fake?   Your carefully crafted persona of practiced aloofness, bitchiness would crumble.   Everyone would know you're fragile and the right word(s) spoken at the perfect time will reduce you to tiny fragments. So tiny the slightest breeze will carry you into infinity. But perhaps that would bring relief. The shell you are would scatter into nothingness, but your soul would be free to scream, cry and make its way, hopefully, to an eternity that would be peaceful, forgiving; filling the soul with satisfaction.

If I let this happen, finally I would have escaped this pain that my life has been. I don't know who I am. I have tried so many faces. I just want to be left alone to scream until it shatters the horrors I have endured. The terror that life is at times. But, I don't scream. I'm too aware of my surroundings, common decency and good manners. I can't win this fight. I hold in my scream. Everyone thinks my life is fine, but my inner being is being consumed by the poison within that screams.

The last time I screamed he continued to rape me. My screams of pain and trauma were met with words of "just relax! Calm down! Shut up!" Hence, my screams have been held captive ever since that moment. I don't want to be violated again so I don't scream. I allow myself to be raped of my dignity, my self-respect. I don't know who I am.

**The real me died that night. Resurrection is not an option.**

The hopeful, young me is still on that cold ground on that dark night. Still wondering how did I let this happen to her?

How did I let this man forever alter our lives? This monster who wanted to continue this rape.  What do I do for her?  How can I save her?

# SCREAM!

# About The Author

Timeless was born in Walterboro, SC.  She is a graduate of Walterboro High School and The College of Charleston in Charleston, SC.  She is employed by a Medicaid HMO.  Timeless has one daughter.  She enjoys listening to jazz, Neo-soul, R and B and Gospel music.

Timeless lives by the mantra God, family and career.  She cherishes her network of friends.

Over the years these people have proven to be strong towers whenever necessary.

Timeless loves to laugh and make others laugh. Writing poetry is her passion.  It is the way to say all the things that cannot be said aloud effectively.  She lets God take control of her pen to inspire others; her heart takes control when she writes about love and her mind takes control when she ventures into a world she has

never experienced.  Imagination is everything.
Being authentic is her measuring stick.  She
can always be found with her nose in a book
or a pen in her hand writing, writing, writing.